Fun Fan Facts:
The Unofficial NBA Edition

Denver Nuggets

Everything Young Nuggets Fans Should Know

By: Jake Liam

Dedication

For every Nuggets fan who watched the second round of the draft, heard the name Nikola Jokic, and had absolutely no idea what was coming.

You do now.

THE NBA
BY THE NUMBERS

MOST NBA CHAMPIONSHIPS*

CELTICS (18)
LAKERS (17)
WARRIORS (7)
BULLS (6)
SPURS (5)

As of the 2024-25 Season. † One Trophy = 4 Championships.

NBA HISTORY SNAPSHOT

1946 — NBA Founded
1954 — Shot Clock Introduced
1979 — 3-Point Line Added
2023 — NBA Cup Introduced

BIG NUMBERS

$156 million
Stephen Curry's est. earnings in the 24-25 season

7'7"
Tallest player in NBA history (Gheorghe Mureșan & Manute Bol)

30 | 4 | 82

30 Teams Competing in the NBA

4 Playoff Rounds

82 Games Per Season

DENVER NUGGETS
IN THE NBA

- FOUNDED: 1976 †
- NBA TITLES: 1
- CONFERENCE TITLES: 1*

34 Playoff Appearances

*† Founding dates are complicated & may cause arguments at Thanksgiving. Ask someone born before color TV. All Titles reflect pre-relocation franchise history. * As of 2024-25 Season.*

NBA ALL-TIME MVP LEADERS

KAREEM ABDUL-JABBAR (6) ★ MICHAEL JORDAN (5) ★ BILL RUSSELL (5)

EASTERN CONFERENCE

Atlantic – **Celtics**
Atlantic – **Nets**
Atlantic – **Knicks**
Atlantic – **76ers**
Atlantic – **Raptors**
Central – **Bulls**
Central – **Cavaliers**
Central – **Pistons**
Central – **Pacers**
Central – **Bucks**
Southeast – **Hawks**
Southeast – **Hornets**
Southeast – **Heat**
Southeast – **Magic**
Southeast – **Wizards**

WESTERN CONFERENCE

Pacific – **Lakers**
Pacific – **Clippers**
Pacific – **Warriors**
Pacific – **Suns**
Pacific – **Kings**
Northwest – **Nuggets**
Northwest – **Timberwolves**
Northwest – **Thunder**
Northwest – **Trail Blazers**
Northwest – **Jazz**
Southwest – **Mavericks**
Southwest – **Rockets**
Southwest – **Spurs**
Southwest – **Pelicans**
Southwest – **Grizzlies**

Introduction

Welcome, fans! Whether you're new to cheering for the Denver Nuggets or you've been bleeding the team colors your whole life, this book is packed with fun, exciting facts about your favorite team. Get ready to impress your friends and family with everything you know about the Nuggets.

Quick Timeout

This book is packed with stats. Like, A LOT of stats. Every fact was checked, double-checked, and triple-checked. But here's the thing about basketball history: not everyone agrees on everything. Ask someone who watched games before color TV and someone who grew up with instant replay and you'll get two completely different answers. My dad, stepdad, uncle, and grandpa all argued about the same fact. Four people. Four answers. All of them think they're right. So if you spot something that doesn't match what you've heard, congratulations. You might be a bigger fan than the people who helped make this book. And honestly? That's pretty cool.

HOW IT WORKS

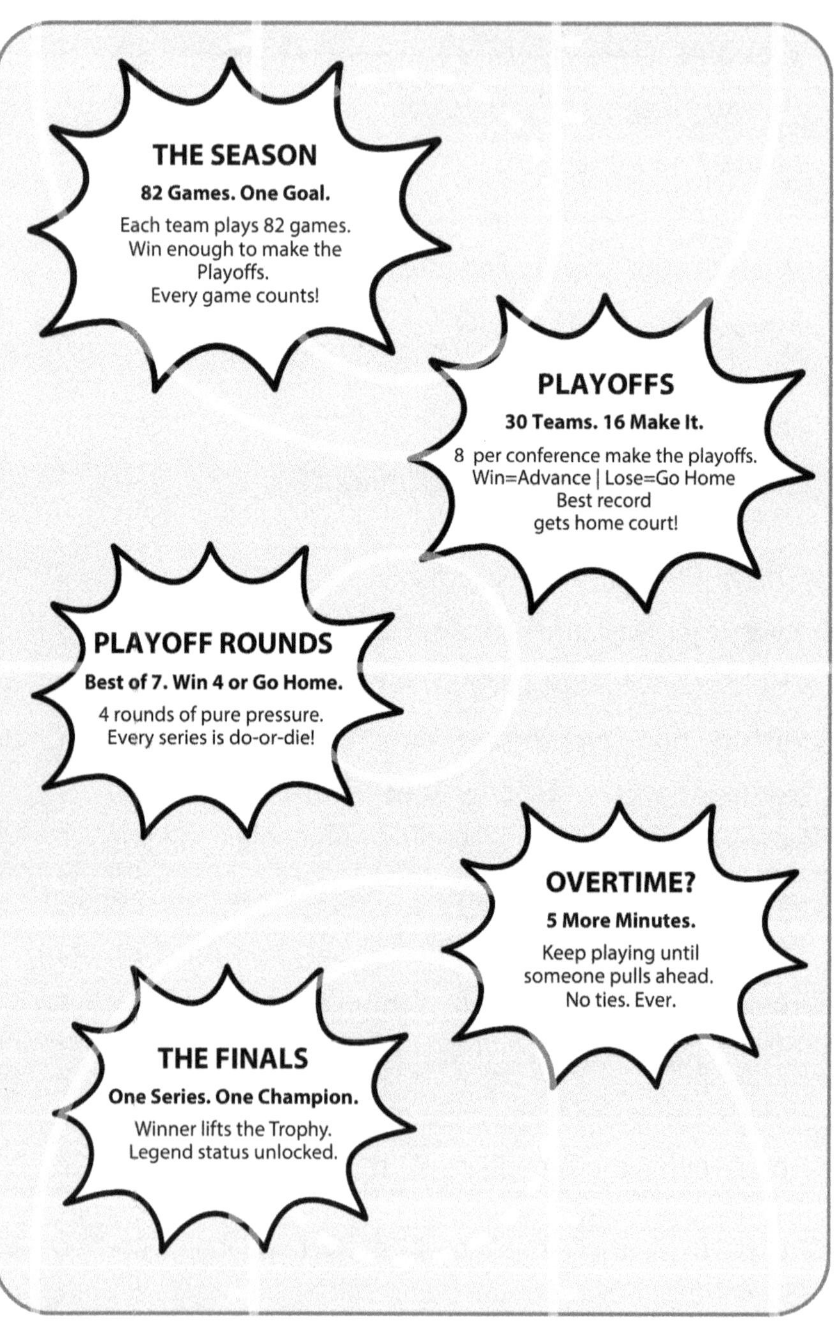

THE SEASON
82 Games. One Goal.
Each team plays 82 games.
Win enough to make the
Playoffs.
Every game counts!

PLAYOFFS
30 Teams. 16 Make It.
8 per conference make the playoffs.
Win=Advance | Lose=Go Home
Best record
gets home court!

PLAYOFF ROUNDS
Best of 7. Win 4 or Go Home.
4 rounds of pure pressure.
Every series is do-or-die!

OVERTIME?
5 More Minutes.
Keep playing until
someone pulls ahead.
No ties. Ever.

THE FINALS
One Series. One Champion.
Winner lifts the Trophy.
Legend status unlocked.

How the NBA Works

At first glance, basketball feels simple. Ten players. One ball. Two hoops. Go.

Then the NBA adds the layers.

An 82-game regular season. A draft where bad teams pick first. Playoffs that last two full months. Superstars who can change everything with one trade. Dynasties that rise, fall, and rise again.

And somehow, it all works.

The NBA is built on one big idea: every team gets a chance to reset, reload, and rise again. No relegation. No dropping down to a lower league. Just basketball, every night, from October through June.

It is a league designed for drama, stars, and comebacks. And once you understand the flow, it is impossible to stop watching.

The League Setup

The NBA has 30 teams, spread across the United States and Canada. Those teams are split into two conferences:

- Eastern Conference
- Western Conference

Each conference has three divisions, mostly based on geography. Divisions matter for scheduling, but not as much as they used to.

Every team plays 82 regular season games, usually from October through April. Home games. Road games. Back-to-back nights. Long road trips. The season is a marathon before the sprint even starts.

Win games, and you climb the standings. Lose too many, and the pressure builds fast.

How Games Are Played

An NBA game has four quarters, each lasting 12 minutes. That means 48 minutes of game time, plus timeouts, free throws, and the occasional coach argument that adds another 20 minutes nobody planned for.

Scoring is simple:

- A shot inside the three-point line is worth 2 points
- A shot beyond the arc is worth 3 points
- Free throws are worth 1 point

If the score is tied at the end of regulation, the game goes to overtime, which lasts 5 minutes. Still tied? Another overtime. Keep going until someone wins.

There is a shot clock too. Teams have 24 seconds to take a shot. No standing around. No holding the ball forever. Keep it moving.

The Regular Season Race

The regular season is long for a reason. It tests everything.

Depth. Health. Focus. Patience.

Teams play opponents from both conferences, but they face conference rivals more often. By the end of the season, each conference's top teams have earned their playoff spots the hard way.

The goal is simple: make the playoffs. But there is a twist.

The NBA Cup

In 2023, the NBA added something new to the middle of the season. Something with actual stakes. They called it the In-Season Tournament, now known as the NBA Cup.

It works like this: Every team plays a small group stage during November and December, with special court designs that look like nothing else in basketball. The best teams advance to a knockout round held in Las Vegas.

The winners split a prize pool. Players earn bonus money. And for the first time, a team could lift a trophy before the playoffs even started.

Some fans are still warming up to it. Some players love it. But the moment a team starts treating it seriously and a crowd shows up buzzing in December, it feels like something.

Which, honestly, sounds about right.

The Play-In Tournament

Instead of sending the top eight teams from each conference straight to the playoffs, the NBA added something new. The Play-In Tournament.

Here is how it works:

- Teams ranked 1 through 6 in each conference are safe
- Teams ranked 7 through 10 fight for the final two playoff spots

The 7 and 8 seeds have an advantage. Win once and you are in. Lose and you still get one more shot. The 9 and 10 seeds have to win twice in a row just to earn a first-round matchup.

It turns the end of the season into a sprint. Every game suddenly matters more. Fans love it. Coaches age rapidly.

The NBA Playoffs

Once the playoffs begin, everything tightens.

Sixteen teams enter. Eight from each conference. Every round is a best-of-seven games series. That means the first team to win four games moves on:

- First Round
- Conference Semifinals
- Conference Finals
- NBA Finals

Home-court advantage matters. Crowds get louder. Rotations get shorter. Superstars play heavier minutes. One bad quarter can flip a series. One great performance can define a career.

By the time the NBA Finals arrive in June, only two teams are left. One from the East. One from the West. Four wins away from a championship. Four wins away from history.

The NBA Draft: Hope Begins Here

Here is where the NBA gets clever. Every summer, new players enter the league through the NBA Draft. Teams take turns selecting college players, international stars, and teenagers straight out of high school.

The teams that finished with the worst records get the best odds to pick early through the Draft Lottery. It is not guaranteed, but it gives struggling franchises a real shot at changing their future with one pick.

That means one bad season does not doom you forever. It might actually change everything. Some franchises are rebuilt by a single draft night moment.

Hope shows up wearing a new jersey.

No Relegation. All Pressure.

Unlike many global sports leagues, NBA teams never drop down to a lower league. They always stay in the NBA.

That does not mean there is no pressure.

Fans remember losing seasons. Owners make changes. Coaches get replaced. Players get traded. Every year is a test of direction, patience, and belief.

Stars, Systems, and Showtime

The NBA is famous for its stars. But stars do not win alone.

Teams need chemistry. Coaches need systems. Role players need to deliver on the biggest stages. One injury. One hot streak. One trade deadline deal. Any of it can flip a season.

That balance between individual brilliance and team basketball is what makes the league special.

Fast breaks. Buzzer-beaters. Game 7s. And moments that get replayed forever. That is the NBA.

Once you get the flow, it is pure electricity.

Denver Nuggets Facts

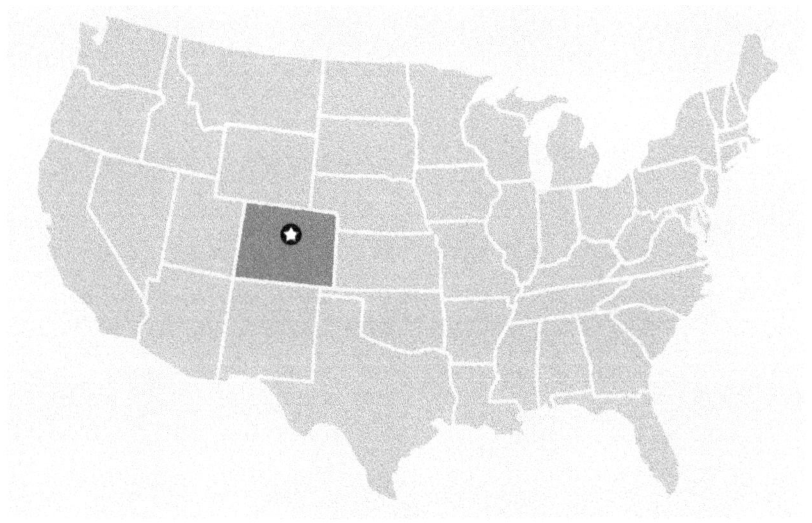

Home City

Denver, Colorado

Metro Area Population

About 2.9 Million

Home Arena

Ball Arena

Arena Capacity

19,520

Conference / Division

Western Conference / Northwest Division

Famous Local Food

Green chile burritos, bison burgers, Rocky Mountain oysters, craft beer

Chapter 1: From the ABA to the Mile High City

1. Three Names Before Breakfast

The Denver Nuggets did not arrive in the world as the Denver Nuggets. They arrived as the Denver Rockets in 1967, which was a perfectly fine name for a team in the American Basketball Association, a league that was itself still figuring out what it wanted to be. The Rockets name lasted about as long as most people's New Year's resolutions. There was already a Houston Rockets in the NBA, which created enough confusion that the team rebranded to the Denver Larks in 1974. The Larks. As in the bird. As in, a decision someone made out loud in a professional meeting and nobody stopped them.

The Larks lasted approximately one season before everyone involved agreed it was not working. The team became the Denver Nuggets in 1974, named after the gold nuggets from Colorado's famous mining history, and this time the name stuck. It had local meaning, it had weight, and crucially it did not sound like a bird that gets startled easily. The Nuggets joined the NBA in 1976 when the ABA merged with the established league, bringing Denver onto the biggest basketball stage in the country.

From Rockets to Larks to Nuggets. Every great story has a rough draft. Some have two.

2. The Mile High Advantage Nobody Warned You About

Denver sits at 5,280 feet above sea level. That number is not just a fun trivia fact. It is a physical obstacle that visiting NBA teams run directly into approximately forty-eight minutes into their first game at Ball Arena, usually right around the moment they realize their legs have stopped working properly and nobody told them this was going to happen.

At altitude, the air contains less oxygen per breath. For athletes performing at maximum intensity, this means the body has to work harder to do the same things it does at sea level without a second thought. Visiting players who have not acclimatized to Denver's elevation frequently report feeling heavier, slower, and significantly more tired than usual in the fourth quarter. The Nuggets, who practice and live in Denver year-round, have long since adapted. Their lungs are essentially small, efficient mountain engines at this point.

The altitude advantage is real enough that sports scientists have studied it and coaches have complained about it for decades. Denver fans consider this part of their home court advantage the same way other teams consider a loud crowd or a long road trip. The Nuggets did not design the Rocky Mountains. They just had the good sense to build an arena next to them.

3. Jumping to the Big League

The American Basketball Association was one of the more charismatic experiments in sports history. It had a red, white, and blue basketball, a three-point line before the NBA thought that was a good idea, and a collection of genuinely talented players performing in a league that never quite got the respect it deserved. The Denver Nuggets were one of its better teams, which meant that when the ABA folded in 1976 and four of its franchises merged into the NBA, Denver was in a strong position to make the jump.

The merger brought the Nuggets, the Indiana Pacers, the New York Nets, and the San Antonio Spurs into the NBA. Denver arrived with an established fanbase, a competitive roster, and David Thompson, one of the most explosive players anyone had ever seen. More on

Thompson in Chapter 2. The transition from ABA to NBA meant facing tougher competition every single night, but the Nuggets had spent nearly a decade building something real and they were not intimidated by the upgrade in competition.

Denver has been an NBA city ever since, which is easy to forget given how long the franchise spent being competitive but not quite a champion. The 1976 arrival was the foundation. Everything else was built on top of it, slowly, patiently, and occasionally with a very bad uniform decision along the way.

4. Ball Arena and the Fans Who Fill It

Ball Arena opened in 1999 and has gone through several names over the years, cycling through corporate sponsors the way most of us cycle through phone upgrades. It has been the Pepsi Center, it has been Ball Arena, and it has been the home of some of the loudest and most underappreciated fans in the NBA regardless of what the sign on the outside said.

Denver crowds have a reputation for showing up. The city is not one of the massive coastal markets that generates automatic national attention, which means Nuggets fans have spent decades watching their team get overlooked while rooting harder than most. When Denver won the NBA Championship in 2023, the celebration was not just about the trophy. It was about decades of investment in a franchise that took its time getting there and finally delivered.

The arena sits in downtown Denver near Coors Field and has become a central piece of the city's sports infrastructure. On a full night with the crowd locked in and Nikola Jokic doing something that makes the entire building gasp simultaneously, Ball Arena is one of the better places in the NBA to watch a basketball game. The altitude helps with the atmosphere too. Everything feels slightly more intense when everyone in the building is breathing a little harder than usual.

5. The Uniforms: A Journey Through Some Choices

The Denver Nuggets have had some of the most memorable uniforms in NBA history, and memorable is doing a lot of work in that sentence. The original rainbow skyline jerseys from the 1980s featured a multicolored gradient across the chest with a Denver city skyline, and they were so aggressively of their era that they have since become beloved in the way that only truly committed fashion disasters eventually become beloved.

Those jerseys were replaced over the years as the team cycled through cleaner, more conventional looks. Navy blue arrived. The mountain logo appeared. The color scheme settled into something that felt more aligned with Colorado's identity as a place of rugged natural beauty rather than a place where someone spilled a box of crayons on a shirt. The current uniforms are sharp, clean, and built around a mountain peak logo that communicates exactly where this team comes from.

The rainbow skyline jerseys are now sold as retro throwbacks, which means the uniforms that were eventually abandoned as too much are now celebrated as a piece of franchise history. Fashion works in cycles.

The Nuggets in particular seem to work in very colorful ones.

6. David Thompson: Skywalker (1975-1982)

Before anyone had invented a term for what David Thompson could do in the air, David Thompson was already doing it. He arrived in Denver via the ABA in 1975 as one of the most physically gifted players the sport had ever produced, possessing a vertical leap so extraordinary that teammates, opponents, and coaches regularly ran out of adjectives trying to describe it. The nickname Skywalker was not a compliment. It was a straight factual description of what he appeared to be doing when he elevated near the basket.

Thompson was a four-time All-Star and one of the primary reasons Denver basketball mattered in the late 1970s. He could score from anywhere, move in ways that made opponents look like they were playing in a different sport, and carry a team on nights when nothing else was working. On April 9, 1978, he scored 73 points in a single game against Detroit, chasing the single-game scoring record in real time before finishing just short of it. More on that remarkable night in Chapter 3.

His career ended earlier than it should have, derailed by personal struggles that cost him some of his best years. What he left behind was a body of work that Nuggets fans of a certain age still describe with the particular reverence reserved for players who made them feel like anything was possible on a basketball court.

7. Alex English: The Quiet Assassin (1980-1990)

Alex English scored more points than almost anyone who has ever played in the NBA and somehow spent most of his career being treated like a mild surprise rather than a genuine superstar. He averaged over 25 points per game eight seasons in a row for Denver. Eight. In a row. He led the entire NBA in scoring for the decade of the 1980s, which is a fact that still catches people off guard when they hear it because English never generated the national headlines his production deserved.

He was smooth rather than explosive, efficient rather than flashy, and he had a shooting form so silky and repeatable that opposing coaches spent years trying to figure out how to slow it down without ever quite succeeding. He made eight All-Star teams, won the scoring title in 1983, and built the kind of career that looks even more impressive the closer you look at the actual numbers rather than the reputation.

English eventually had his number 2 retired by the Nuggets and was inducted into the Basketball Hall of Fame in 1997, which gave him the belated recognition his playing days sometimes failed to deliver. Denver fans never needed the Hall of Fame to tell them what they already knew. They had watched him score on everybody for a decade and had been trying to explain it to people ever since.

8. Dan Issel: The Horse (1975-1985)

Dan Issel arrived in Denver from the ABA Kentucky Colonels as part of the franchise's foundational generation, and he spent the next decade being the kind of player that every successful team needs but not every team is lucky enough to have. He was not the flashiest Nugget. He was simply the one who showed up every single night, did the work, scored the points, grabbed the rebounds, and made everything around him more functional just by being on the floor.

Issel scored over 27,000 combined ABA and NBA points across his career, a total that puts him among the highest-scoring players in professional basketball history when both leagues are counted together. He was a six-time All-Star, a reliable inside presence in an era when inside presence was harder to come by than anyone admitted, and the franchise's all-time leading scorer for decades until the records eventually started falling to the next generation.

His nickname, The Horse, captured something real about how he played. He was not going to do anything that made the highlight reel specifically because it looked cool. He was going to work. He was going to be there in the fourth quarter when the game needed someone who had not spent the previous three quarters saving their energy for a dramatic moment. The Nuggets retired his number 44, and the city of Denver named him one of its most important sports figures. The Horse ran his race and never stopped.

9. Carmelo Anthony: Melo in Denver (2003-2011)

Carmelo Anthony arrived in Denver as the third overall pick in the 2003 NBA Draft, which is the same draft that produced LeBron James and Dwyane Wade, which gives you some sense of the company he was keeping and the expectations he was carrying from the first day he put on a Nuggets uniform. He handled it fine. Better than fine, actually.

Melo spent eight seasons in Denver becoming one of the purest scorers the league had seen in years. He won the NBA scoring title in the 2006 season, averaged over 26 points per game for most of his Nuggets tenure, and helped build a culture that eventually got Denver to the Western Conference Finals in 2009, the franchise's deepest playoff run in decades. The city loved him in a way that made the ending considerably more complicated.

In the final stretch of his time in Denver, it became clear that Anthony wanted to play elsewhere, a situation that was handled with varying degrees of grace by everyone involved and ended with a trade to the New York Knicks in 2011. More on what Carmelo built specifically in Chapter 3. What belongs here is the full picture of a player who gave Denver some of the most entertaining offensive basketball the city had seen, and who left a fanbase feeling the particular complicated emotion of someone who loved you and then left.

10. Nikola Jokic: The Joker (2015-present)

There is a moment in the 2014 NBA Draft where the broadcast cuts away from draft coverage to air a Taco Bell commercial. When it comes back, Nikola Jokic has been selected by the Denver Nuggets with the 41st overall pick. The 41st pick. A player who would go on to win three NBA MVP awards, one Finals MVP, and one NBA Championship was selected during a fast food advertisement. This fact will never stop being funny.

Jokic grew up in Sombor, Serbia, where he was reportedly more interested in horses than basketball until relatively late in his development. He arrived in Denver looking more like a friendly geology professor than a future MVP, and he proceeded to become the most complete basketball player on the planet so gradually and so quietly that some people did not fully process it until he was already holding the trophy.

He does not dunk often. He does not trash talk. He does not celebrate. He simply sees the game operating about three seconds ahead of everyone else and makes decisions that only make sense after they have already happened. More on what he has accomplished specifically in Chapters 3 and 5. What belongs here is the baseline understanding: the best player in Denver Nuggets history, and one of the best players in the history of the sport, was available at pick 41 because everyone else passed on him. Twice. The Nuggets would like to thank them all personally.

Nikola Jokic celebrates with fans during the Denver Nuggets' 2023 championship parade. The passing wizard from Serbia helped deliver Denver's first NBA title, and the whole city showed up to party. *Photo: Denver Nuggets 2023 Championship Parade (2023). Source: Wikimedia Commons.*

Chapter 3: The Moments That Shook the Mountains

11. Mutombo and the Shot Heard Across Colorado (1994)

The 1994 first-round NBA Playoffs series between the Denver Nuggets and the Seattle SuperSonics is one of the greatest upsets in playoff history, and it happened so fast and so completely that Seattle fans are still processing it. The SuperSonics had finished the regular season with the second-best record in the Western Conference. The Nuggets were the eighth seed. This was not supposed to be a series. It was supposed to be a brief inconvenience for Seattle on the way to something more important.

Denver won three games to two. Dikembe Mutombo, the seven-foot-two defensive force who had come to the Nuggets in 1991, was at the center of everything. He blocked shots, altered the entire Seattle offense, and made the paint feel like a place where bad things happened to good intentions. When Denver closed out the series, Mutombo collapsed to the floor in tears, clutching the basketball, in one of the most genuinely emotional moments in NBA playoff history. He had just helped one of the biggest upsets the sport had seen in years, and he knew exactly what it meant.

The Nuggets became the first eight seed to ever defeat a one seed in a playoff series. Denver celebrated. Seattle did not. Mutombo kept the basketball.

12. David Thompson's 73-Point Night

On the final day of the 1977-78 regular season, David Thompson did something that had never been done before and has barely been approached since. He scored 73 points in a game against the Detroit Pistons, chasing the single-game NBA scoring record held by Wilt Chamberlain in a performance that required the kind of total offensive commitment that makes coaches cover their eyes and fans forget to breathe.

Thompson reached 73 in part because his team needed him to for statistical tiebreaker reasons involving the scoring title race. He knew going in that he needed to score as many points as possible, which freed him to do something most players never get permission to do: just shoot every time he touched the ball and let the number climb wherever it wanted to go. He scored 32 points in the first quarter alone. He finished with 73 and came within a handful of Chamberlain's all-time record of 100.

He did not win the scoring title that season. San Antonio's George Gervin played later that same day, found out what Thompson had scored, and proceeded to put up 63 points of his own to edge him out. Two players scoring over 60 points on the same day to settle a scoring race is a sentence that sounds made up and is completely true. Denver lost the tiebreaker but gained a legendary story.

13. The 2023 NBA Championship: It Was Always Going to Be Denver

The Denver Nuggets won their first NBA Championship on June 12, 2023, defeating the Miami Heat four games to one in a Finals that was less a contest than a demonstration. Nikola Jokic averaged 30 points, 14 rebounds, and 7 assists per game against Miami, numbers so complete and so consistent across five games that opposing coaches were running out of adjustments to try by the third quarter of most of them.

The championship was notable for how it was built. The Nuggets had no major free agent signings, no blockbuster trades, and no moment where a superstar arrived from outside to fix things. Every significant player on the roster had been drafted, developed, and kept in Denver through years of patient, unglamorous roster construction. Jokic was the 41st pick. Jamal Murray was the seventh. Michael Porter Jr. was a draft-night gamble on a player with injury history. Aaron Gordon came via trade but fit the culture like he had always been there.

Denver fans had waited since 1976 for a championship. They celebrated as people celebrate when something they have been hoping for a very long time finally arrives. Loudly. In the mountains. In a building where the altitude makes everything feel slightly more intense than it would anywhere else. It was appropriate.

14. Jamal Murray's Bubble Masterpiece

The 2020 NBA Playoffs took place in the Orlando bubble, a controlled environment created to allow the season to continue safely during a public health crisis. The conditions were strange, the atmosphere was artificial, and Jamal Murray responded by playing some of the most spectacular playoff basketball anyone had seen in years, apparently deciding that the unusual circumstances were an excellent reason to be excellent.

Murray averaged 26.5 points per game through the bubble playoffs and produced multiple individual performances that made NBA fans forget there was no crowd in the building. His 50-point game against the Utah Jazz in the second round was the kind of performance that turns a good player into a remembered player, full of contested pull-up jumpers, difficult finishes, and moments where he simply refused to let the game go in the wrong direction. He also scored 42 points in a game during that same series, meaning he dropped 50 and 42 in back-to-back playoff performances against the same team.

Murray was 23 years old during the bubble playoffs. He played like someone who had been waiting his entire life for exactly this kind of stage and had been quietly preparing for it in a gym somewhere while everyone else was looking in a different direction.

15. Jokic's Christmas Gift to the Rest of Us (2025)

On Christmas Day 2025, Nikola Jokic played a basketball game against the Minnesota Timberwolves and produced a statistical line that had never appeared in an NBA box score before in the history of the league. He scored 55 points. He grabbed 15 rebounds. He dished 15 assists. In one game. Against a good team. On national television. On Christmas Day, which is when the NBA puts its best product on display and Jokic apparently treats as a personal invitation to do something that requires a new category.

A 55-15-15 game had never been done before. Not by Wilt Chamberlain. Not by Oscar Robertson. Not by Michael Jordan or LeBron James or anyone else who had ever played the sport at its highest level. Jokic did it on a holiday while millions of people watched their televisions and tried to explain to family members who do not follow basketball why the large Serbian man was making the commentators sound like they were witnessing a natural disaster.

The truly remarkable detail is that this was not even considered shocking by people who watch Jokic regularly. They saw the final line, nodded, and thought something like yes, that tracks. That is the level Nikola

Jokic has reached. The bar has been moved so high that the rest of the basketball world is still looking for it.

Chapter 4: Altitude, Attitude, and Pure Nuggets Weirdness

16. Rocky the Mascot: Part Athlete, Part Chaos Agent

Rocky the Mountain Lion has been the Denver Nuggets' mascot since 1990 and has spent every year since then attempting to give arena staff cardiac episodes. He is not a mascot who waves at children from a safe distance. He is a mascot who performs backflips off trampolines, rappels from the rafters, and has been known to arrive on court via zipline with the casual energy of someone who does this every Tuesday because they do.

Rocky is consistently ranked among the best mascots in professional sports, which is a category that rewards creativity, athleticism, and a complete absence of personal fear. He has all three in abundance. His pregame and halftime routines have included stunts that would be impressive for a trained gymnast and are genuinely bewildering for a person wearing a large foam mountain lion head. The head does not appear to slow him down at all.

Denver fans treat Rocky as a genuine piece of the game day experience rather than an intermission act, which is the highest compliment a mascot can receive. He has been doing this for over three decades and shows no signs of considering a calmer career path. Somewhere there is a retirement plan for Rocky that nobody has told Rocky about yet.

17. The Altitude Effect: Denver's Invisible Sixth Man

Every visiting team that comes to Ball Arena faces the same opponent that does not appear anywhere on the roster and cannot be guarded, schemed against, or talked out of showing up. The altitude does not care how many championships you have won. It does not care that you are LeBron James. It just quietly removes a percentage of the oxygen from every breath and waits to see what happens in the fourth quarter.

The science is straightforward. At 5,280 feet, the air is thinner and contains less oxygen per breath than at sea level. Athletes performing at maximum intensity feel this most acutely, particularly in the legs, which are the first thing to go when oxygen delivery gets slightly less efficient. Players who live and train in Denver have adapted over time. Players who fly in from sea level cities have not, and the Nuggets have beaten teams in the fourth quarter for decades in ways that can only be partially explained by basketball.

Visiting coaches have been complaining about this officially and unofficially since Denver entered the NBA. The Nuggets have responded to these complaints by continuing to play at 5,280 feet, which is the correct response. You cannot move a mountain. You can, however, build a very good basketball team next to one and let nature handle the rest.

18. The Rainbow Skyline Jerseys: History's Most Lovable Mistake

In the 1980s, the Denver Nuggets wore uniforms that looked like someone had asked a very enthusiastic child to design a professional basketball jersey and then actually went ahead and used the design. The rainbow skyline uniforms featured a multicolored horizontal stripe across the chest in red, gold, blue, yellow, and green, with a Denver city skyline silhouetted inside it. They were loud. They were busy. They were absolutely, completely, unapologetically a lot.

At the time, some people thought they were too much. Those people were not entirely wrong. But something interesting happens to bold fashion decisions over time, particularly in sports. The jerseys that seemed excessive in 1985 become the jerseys that fans want on a retro t-shirt in 2005 and pay serious money for on resale sites in 2025. The rainbow skyline uniforms followed this exact trajectory with precision.

The Nuggets have brought back elements of the rainbow design in various throwback and alternate uniform releases over the years, always to significant fan enthusiasm. What was once considered a visual miscalculation is now considered a piece of franchise identity worth celebrating. The moral of the story is that if you commit hard enough to a questionable decision, time will eventually come around to your side. Fashion takes patience.

19. The Taco Bell Draft Story

The 2014 NBA Draft was proceeding normally until the Denver Nuggets made the best decision in franchise history while the television broadcast was airing a Taco Bell commercial. With the 41st pick, buried deep in the second round while the cameras were pointed somewhere else, Denver selected Nikola Jokic from Mega Leks in Serbia. The pick was announced. The broadcast returned. Nobody outside of Denver's front office treated it as a significant moment.

This is because nobody outside of Denver's front office knew what they had just witnessed. Jokic was not a highly touted prospect. He was a wide-bodied Serbian big man who moved slowly and did not test particularly well athletically. What the Nuggets had identified, through film work and their own evaluation process, was that he could do things with a basketball that had no established category yet. He could pass like a point guard, score like a forward, and read the entire floor like someone standing above it looking down.

Thirty teams passed on Jokic at least once. Twenty of them passed on him twice since he was available in both rounds. The Nuggets selected him during a commercial break and eventually watched him become a three-time MVP. The Taco Bell commercial has not commented publicly on its role in NBA history, but it should probably get some kind of credit.

20. Denver: The Sports City That Plays Outside First

Denver is not a city that sits still. It is a city of hikers, skiers, snowboarders, climbers, and outdoor enthusiasts who treat the Rocky Mountains as a backyard and consider a weekend without fresh air a weekend wasted. This shapes what sports fandom looks like in Colorado in ways that are genuinely different from basketball-first cities like Boston or Chicago.

Nuggets fans love their team, but they love it alongside a full roster of other passions. The Broncos, the Rockies, the Avalanche, and the mountains themselves all compete for Denver's attention in a market that distributes its loyalty across a wider landscape than most. This used to be cited as a weakness for Denver sports franchises. The fanbase was considered too diffuse, too spread out, too easily distracted by a powder day to fully commit to a basketball team.

Then the Nuggets won a championship in 2023 and the entire city showed up to celebrate in a way that made it very clear the commitment had been there all along, waiting for a reason to fully express itself. Denver does not love loudly every single day. It loves deeply and then finds a very large occasion when it needs to. The championship parade through downtown confirmed that Denver's sports culture was never absent. It was just also wearing ski boots.

21. How You Build a Champion Without Buying One

The 2023 NBA Championship was won by a team that had not signed a single marquee free agent to build around and had not traded for a superstar to push them over the top. Every meaningful piece of the championship roster arrived through the draft, through patient development, or through smart complementary trades that fit the culture rather than disrupting it. In an era when superteams and blockbuster free agent signings dominate the conversation, Denver won a title by doing things the slow, unglamorous, absolutely correct way.

Nikola Jokic was the 41st pick. Jamal Murray was seventh overall. Michael Porter Jr. was a developmental gamble on a player with a significant injury history who took years to fully realize his potential. Aaron Gordon came via trade from Orlando in 2021, a move that completed the lineup without breaking the chemistry that had been building for years. Christian Braun was a first-round pick who developed into a dependable starter.

The lesson Denver's championship offers to every franchise that wants to copy it is also the reason most franchises will not copy it. Patience is genuinely difficult. Trusting a draft pick who was selected during a Taco Bell commercial to become the best player in the world requires either extraordinary scouting or extraordinary faith or some combination of both. Denver had both. The trophy is the evidence.

22. Three MVPs and the Case for the Best Player Alive

Nikola Jokic has won three NBA Most Valuable Player awards. He has also finished second in MVP voting twice, meaning that in five consecutive seasons he was considered either the best or second best player in the entire league. For context, only Kareem Abdul-Jabbar, Michael Jordan, LeBron James, and Bill Russell have won three or more MVP awards in NBA history. Jokic joined that group at age 27.

What makes Jokic's MVPs different from most is the way he earns them. Most MVP players dominate through one primary skill that becomes impossible to stop. Jokic dominates through everything simultaneously. He leads his team in scoring, rebounds, and assists on most nights, which is something that simply does not happen with other players at the center position. He became the first big man in NBA history to average a triple-double for an entire season, posting 29.6 points, 12.7 rebounds, and 10.2 assists per game in 2024-25.

His Christmas Day 55-15-15 performance in 2025 added another entry to a highlight reel that somehow keeps getting longer. Every time a reasonable person looks at the numbers and thinks Jokic has probably done everything there is to do, he does something that required a new line in the record books. The Nuggets picked him 41st. The 40 teams that passed on him are still thinking about it.

23. The Pieces Around the Joker

A great supporting cast does not announce itself. It simply makes the best player better and handles the nights when the best player needs help. The Nuggets have built one of the more effective supporting structures in the league around Nikola Jokic, and the pieces have shifted and evolved as the team's needs have changed.

Jamal Murray remains Denver's co-star and the player most capable of taking over a game independently when the situation demands it. His playoff performances have established him as one of the most dangerous postseason scorers in the league, a player who elevates specifically when the games get harder. Cameron Johnson arrived in the 2025 offseason, adding shooting and versatility to a lineup that needed both. Aaron Gordon provides the defensive anchor and the kind of selfless, winning-first presence that championship teams require. Christian Braun developed from a draft pick into a starter who competes every night without complaint.

Jonas Valanciunas joined as the best backup center Jokic has played alongside in Denver, giving the coaching staff actual rotation options at the position for the first time in years. The roster is deep, balanced, and constructed around the specific things Jokic needs to operate at his best. That is not an accident. That is a front office that has learned from watching the same player for a decade exactly what he needs to do what he does.

24. New Coach, Same Mountain

When the Nuggets fired head coach Michael Malone and general manager Calvin Booth with three games remaining in the 2024-25 regular season, the basketball world paid attention. Malone had been with Denver since 2015. He had coached the team through the championship run. Firing him before the season was even officially over was the kind of decisive, uncomfortable move that organizations make when they believe something needs to change and are willing to absorb the awkwardness of the timing.

David Adelman was hired as head coach in May 2025 and immediately faced the challenge that every new Nuggets coach faces: how do you coach a player who is already making the right decision before you have finished designing the play? The answer Adelman arrived at was essentially to build the system around Jokic's instincts rather than alongside them, giving him the freedom to operate while installing structure for the moments when structure matters.

The early results were encouraging. Denver entered the 2025-26 season with a healthier roster, a cleaner rotation, and a coach who had earned the trust of the locker room quickly. Adelman's first season has shown a team that retained its identity while finding new ways to express it. The mountain does not move. The team keeps finding better routes to the top.

25. The Window That Will Not Close

The Denver Nuggets are in an unusual position for a team that has already won a championship. Their best player is 30 years old, which in most situations would prompt a conversation about contention windows and ticking clocks. With Nikola Jokic, the conversation is more complicated, because Jokic has never been an athlete whose value depended on youth and explosiveness. He has always been a thinker operating inside a body, and thinkers tend to age better than leapers.

The roster around him is young enough to grow and experienced enough to compete now. Jamal Murray, Christian Braun, and Cameron Johnson are all in their mid-twenties. The team has cap flexibility heading into future offseasons and a front office that has proven it can find value where other teams overlook it. Denver is not rebuilding. Denver is not declining. Denver is a franchise in the middle of a window that opened in 2023 and shows no clear signs of closing.

For a city that waited nearly five decades for its first championship, the idea of sustained contention feels almost unreasonably good. Nuggets fans have earned the right to expect this. They live at 5,280 feet, they share their air with every visiting team, and they have Nikola Jokic running their offense. The rest of the league is welcome to come to Denver and try to stop it. They should probably acclimatize first.

Bonus Trivia Quiz!

You think you are a true Nuggets fan? Try this bonus quiz!

1. What were the Denver Nuggets originally called when they launched in 1967?

A) The Denver Miners
B) The Denver Rockets
C) The Denver Larks
D) The Colorado Peaks

2. At what elevation does Ball Arena sit, giving the Nuggets their famous altitude advantage?

A) 4,200 feet
B) 4,800 feet
C) 5,280 feet
D) 6,000 feet

3. Which four ABA franchises merged into the NBA in 1976?

A) Denver, Kentucky, New York, Indiana
B) Denver, Indiana, New York Nets, San Antonio
C) Denver, Virginia, Utah, Memphis
D) Denver, Carolina, New York Nets, Kentucky

4. What was David Thompson's nickname, earned for his extraordinary leaping ability?

A) The Rocket

B) The Condor

C) Skywalker

D) Air Thompson

5. How many consecutive seasons did Alex English average over 25 points per game for Denver?

A) Five

B) Six

C) Seven

D) Eight

6. What was Dan Issel's nickname?

A) The Bull

B) The Horse

C) The Engine

D) The Bear

7. With which overall pick did the Denver Nuggets select Nikola Jokic in the 2014 NBA Draft?

A) 15th

B) 27th

C) 35th

D) 41st

8. What was happening on the TV broadcast at the exact moment Jokic was drafted?

A) A halftime show
B) A Taco Bell commercial
C) A weather update
D) An interview with the commissioner

9. The 1994 Nuggets became the first eighth seed to ever beat a first seed in the playoffs. Who did they defeat?

A) The Utah Jazz
B) The Los Angeles Lakers
C) The Seattle SuperSonics
D) The Phoenix Suns

10. How many points did Jamal Murray score in his iconic bubble playoff game against the Utah Jazz?

A) 40
B) 45
C) 50
D) 55

11. In what year did the Denver Nuggets win their first NBA Championship?

A) 2021
B) 2022
C) 2023
D) 2024

12. What record did Nikola Jokic set on Christmas Day 2025?

A) First player to score 60 points in a Christmas game
B) First player in NBA history to record a 55-15-15 game
C) First center to win five MVP awards
D) First player to record 25 assists in a single game

13. Which opposing team did Jokic achieve his Christmas Day record against?

A) Golden State Warriors
B) Los Angeles Lakers
C) Minnesota Timberwolves
D) Oklahoma City Thunder

14. Who replaced Michael Malone as Denver's head coach ahead of the 2025-26 season?

A) Mike D'Antoni

B) David Adelman

C) Jason Kidd

D) Nate McMillan

15. Which player did Denver acquire to add shooting and versatility ahead of the 2025-26 season?

A) Mikal Bridges

B) Cameron Johnson

C) Ben Simmons

D) Dorian Finney-Smith

Super Fan Secret Challenge

Only a true Nuggets fan will know this.

(No Answer Provided)

In the ABA, the Denver franchise briefly used a different name before settling on the Nuggets in 1974. What was the short-lived name they used?

A) The Denver Larks
B) The Denver Miners
C) The Denver Peaks
D) The Colorado Rockets

Answer Key

1. B) The Denver Rockets

2. C) 5,280 feet

3. B) Denver, Indiana, New York Nets, San Antonio

4. C) Skywalker

5. D) Eight

6. B) The Horse

7. D) 41st

8. B) A Taco Bell commercial

9. C) The Seattle SuperSonics

10. C) 50

11. C) 2023

12. B) First player in NBA history to record a 55-15-15 game

13. C) Minnesota Timberwolves

14. B) David Adelman

15. B) Cameron Johnson

NBA PLAYOFF BRACKET

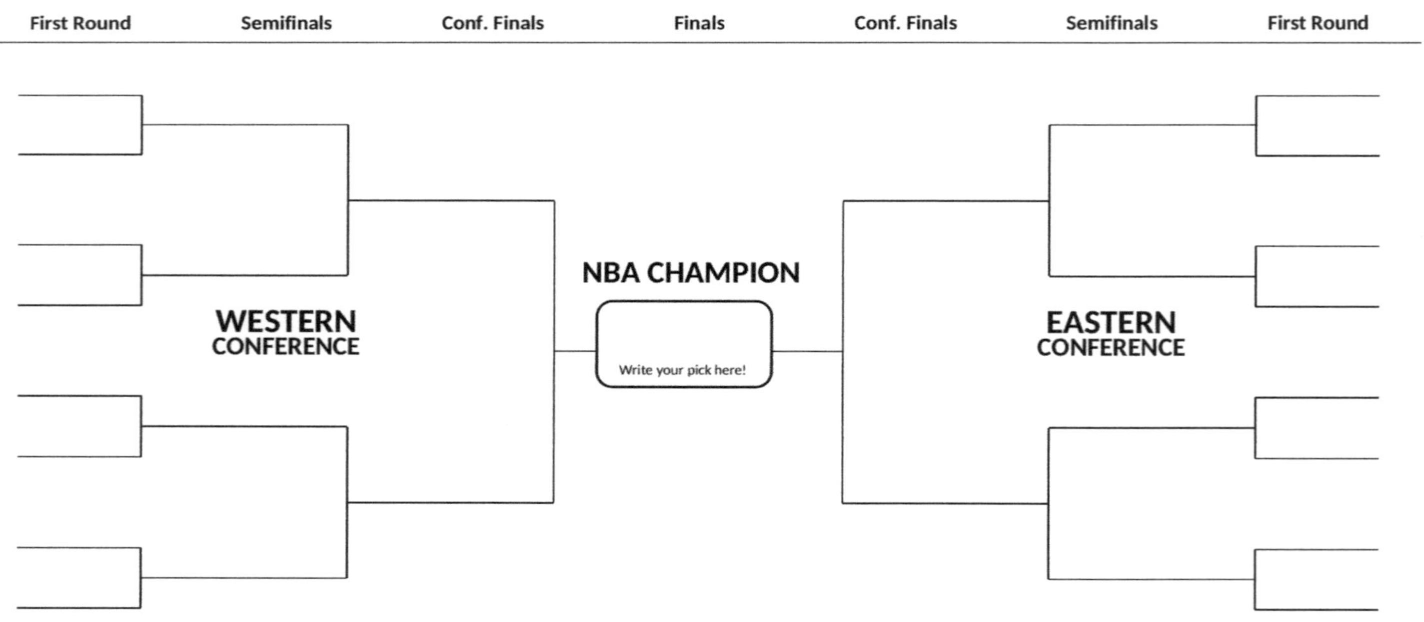

* Fill in your picks and try not to argue with your friends about it!

Part of the Fun Fan Facts: The Unofficial Sports Guide Series

Be the Boss of the Playoffs

You've broken down the matchups. You know which superstar takes over in the fourth quarter. You've seen the bench units that quietly decide series. You've watched the adjustments coaches make when their backs are against the wall.

Now it's time to stop watching and start deciding.

On this page, you are not just a fan. You are the Head Coach drawing up the last play with three seconds left on the clock. You are the GM who built this roster. You are the analyst who saw it all coming.

This is not just filling out a bracket.

This is building your championship run.

Sixteen teams enter the NBA Playoffs. The path is brutal. Best of seven. No shortcuts. No hiding. Every round gets louder, harder, and more personal.

This bracket is your Playoff Control Room.

The Game Plan

1. Survive Round One: Start with the opening round. Which matchup is going seven games? Who has the closer? Who folds under pressure? Make the calls.

2. Feel the Momentum: As you move into the Conference Semifinals and Conference Finals, things change. Role players become heroes. Stars feel the weight. Trust your reads.

3. Own the Finals: Trace your picks all the way to the NBA Finals. When the confetti falls and the trophy is raised, you'll find out who earned it.

House Rules: Circle your boldest upset. That is your official "I knew it" moment.

Choose Your Weapon: Pencil if you want flexibility. Pen if you trust your instincts. Sharpie if you believe in chaos.

Because once the playoffs tip off, there is no rewinding Game 7.

Make your picks. Trust your basketball brain. And let the playoff drama begin.

Fun Facts Wrap-Up

You made it through! You're officially a true superfan! Now it's time to put your knowledge to the test. Share these facts with friends and see who really knows their team best.

Love the series?

Your reviews help other fans discover Fun Fan Facts. If you enjoyed this book, we'd really appreciate you sharing your thoughts and leaving a review.

Want more Fun Fan Facts?

Scan the QR code below to visit our site and explore bonus trivia, challenges, and special extras - including new teams, future series, and collectible fun as they're released.

Collect All the Fun Fan Facts Series!

Check off every book you read. See the full set on Amazon. Search "Fun Fan Facts Jake Liam."

World Cup 2026 Edition

☐ Algeria   ☐ Scotland   ☐ Morocco
☐ France   ☐ Brazil   ☐ Switzerland
☐ Paraguay   ☐ Ivory Coast   ☐ Curaçao
☐ Argentina   ☐ Senegal   ☐ Netherlands
☐ Germany   ☐ Canada   ☐ Tunisia
☐ Portugal   ☐ Japan   ☐ Ecuador
☐ Australia   ☐ South Africa   ☐ New Zealand
☐ Ghana   ☐ Cape Verde   ☐ United States
☐ Qatar   ☐ Jordan   ☐ Egypt
☐ Austria   ☐ South Korea   ☐ Norway
☐ Haiti   ☐ Colombia   ☐ Uruguay
☐ Saudi Arabia   ☐ Mexico   ☐ England
☐ Belgium   ☐ Spain   ☐ Panama
☐ Iran   ☐ Croatia   ☐ Uzbekistan

World Cup 2026 Group Edition

☐ Group A   ☐ Group F   ☐ Group K
☐ Group E   ☐ Group J   ☐ Group D
☐ Group I   ☐ Group C   ☐ Group H
☐ Group B   ☐ Group G   ☐ Group L

English Football Edition

☐ Arsenal F.C. ☐ Manchester City

☐ Aston Villa F.C. ☐ Manchester United

☐ Chelsea F.C. ☐ Newcastle United F.C.

☐ Everton F.C. ☐ Tottenham Hotspur

☐ Fulham F.C. ☐ West Ham United

☐ Liverpool F.C. ☐ Wrexham A.F.C.

NBA Edition

☐ Atlanta Hawks ☐ Miami Heat

☐ Boston Celtics ☐ Milwaukee Bucks

☐ Brooklyn Nets ☐ Minnesota Timberwolves

☐ Charlotte Hornets ☐ New Orleans Pelicans

☐ Chicago Bulls ☐ New York Knicks

☐ Cleveland Cavaliers ☐ Oklahoma City Thunder

☐ Dallas Mavericks ☐ Orlando Magic

☐ Denver Nuggets ☐ Philadelphia 76ers

☐ Detroit Pistons ☐ Phoenix Suns

☐ Golden State Warriors ☐ Portland Trail Blazers

☐ Houston Rockets ☐ Sacramento Kings

☐ Indiana Pacers ☐ San Antonio Spurs

☐ LA Clippers ☐ Toronto Raptors

☐ Los Angeles Lakers ☐ Utah Jazz

☐ Memphis Grizzlies ☐ Washington Wizards

About the Author

Jake is a 13-year-old sports fan who loves football, American football, and basketball. He plays soccer as a goalie and dreams of one day playing for West Ham United and helping teach kids to love the game. His passion for sports runs in the family - his dad was a professional baseball player, and his stepdad sparked his love for West Ham. Through the Fun Fan Facts series, he shares the fun and excitement of sports with fans everywhere.

www.ingramcontent.com/pod-product-compliance
Lightning Source LLC
Chambersburg PA
CBHW050040040726
47599CB00015B/1774